modern readers

stage 1

The Secret of the Pyramid

Eduardo Amos
Elisabeth Prescher

2nd edition

Richmond

Diretoria: *Paul Berry*
Gerência editorial: *Sandra Possas*
Coordenação de revisão: *Estevam Vieira Lédo Jr.*
Coordenação de produção gráfica: *André Monteiro, Maria de Lourdes Rodrigues*
Coordenação de produção industrial: *Wilson Troque*

Projeto editorial: *Kylie Mackin*

Edição e preparação de texto: *Kylie Mackin*
Assistência editorial: *Gabriela Peixoto Vilanova*
Revisão: *Maria Cecília Kinker Caliendo*
Projeto gráfico de miolo e capa: *Ricardo Van Steen Comunicações e Propaganda Ltda./Oliver Fuchs*
Edição de arte: *Christiane Borin*
Ilustrações de miolo e capa: *Victor Tavares*
Diagramação: *Formato Comunicação*
Pré-impressão: *Hélio P. de Souza Filho, Marcio H. Kamoto*
Impressão e acabamento: Log&Print Gráfica e Logística S.A.
Lote: 753563
Código: 12040933

Dados Internacionais de Catalogação na Publicação (CIP)
(Câmara Brasileira do Livro, SP, Brasil)

Amos, Eduardo
The secret of the Pyramid / Eduardo Amos, Elisabeth Prescher. — 2. ed. — São Paulo : Moderna, 2004. — (Modern readers ; stage 1)

1. Inglês (Ensino fundamental) I. Prescher, Elisabeth. II. Título. III. Série.

04-0908 CDD-372.652

Índices para catálogo sistemático:
1. Inglês : Ensino fundamental 372.652

ISBN 85-16-04093-3

Richmond
Santillana Educação Ltda.
Rua Padre Adelino, 758, 3º andar - Belenzinho
São Paulo - SP - Brasil - CEP 03303-904
www.richmond.com.br
2022

Impresso no Brasil

Chapter 1

Claudia Lima and her parents are in Egypt. They're with a group of tourists on their way to the pyramids. A boy is sitting next to Claudia. His name is Dan Arnold.

Claudia – Where are you from?

Dan – I'm American, from Denver. What about you?

Claudia – I'm from Brazil...

Tour Guide – Ladies and gentlemen, on your right, there is the Great Pyramid of Khu-fu. It's about 5,000 years old and it's the biggest pyramid in the valley of Gizeh.

Now the tourists are inside the Great Pyramid.

They enter a small chamber. Claudia and Dan are behind the group. At the back of the chamber, there are two corridors. The tourists go to the right. Dan goes to the left.

Dan – Come on, Claudia! Let's turn left.

Claudia – But our group's in the other corridor.

Dan – Don't worry about them! Maybe there's something interesting to the left.

Claudia – Isn't it dangerous?

Dan – Of course not. Two other guys from our group are entering the corridor too. Look! There they are. Let's go!

Now the kids are inside the passage. But they can't see the men. And there are no doors and no openings.

Claudia and Dan are puzzled.

Claudia – Where are they? They were here a second ago!

Dan – But there are no doors here. There is no way out.

Claudia – Maybe there's a secret door.

Claudia – Look, Dan! Footprints! The two men are behind this wall.

Dan – But how? Where's the door?

Claudia – Here!...This wall is a door!

Dan – Let's open it.

They push the wall and it opens.

Now Claudia and Dan are behind the wall too. They are in a narrow passage. It's long and dark. There are voices at the end of the passage.

Chapter 2

At the end of the passage, there is a large round chamber, with many doors. The two men from the corridor are in the middle of the chamber. They are Doctor Jungen, an archeologist, and his assistant Godron.

Doctor Jungen – According to my calculations, this is the Room of the Seven Doors.

Godron – You're a genius, Doctor Jungen.

Doctor Jungen – We're close, Godron... very close to the Sacred Papyrus of Sekhmet... It's behind one of these doors.

Godron – Fantastic! Doctor, this is a great moment for the universe.

Doctor Jungen – No, this is a great moment for me. The secret of the Pharaohs is almost mine.

Godron – Why is it so important for you?

Doctor Jungen – With the revelations contained in the papyrus, I can have Sekhmet's power! With the papyrus in my hands, I can control the world!

Claudia and Dan are shocked.

Dan – They're thieves, Claudia! Thieves! Let's...

Claudia – Be quiet, Dan! They can hear us.

Doctor Jungen – There is somebody else here!

Doctor Jungen and Godron see the kids. The two men are angry. Claudia and Dan are in trouble.

Doctor Jungen – Don't move! Stay where you are!

Claudia and Dan are prisoners now. They are afraid. They're in a small empty room. All they can see is a tiny hole up on the wall.

Suddenly, a ray of sunlight shines through the hole.

Claudia – Look, Dan! A ray of sunlight! It can help us. We can escape.

Dan – How?

Claudia – Let's use your glasses... Turn around!

In a few minutes, Claudia and Dan are free...

...but they are afraid. The two men are still nearby.

Dan – Let's get out of here. Quick!

Claudia – I can't remember the way out!

Dan – Hmmm. Look, there's a small door at the back of the room. Let's go.

Soon they are in a huge room with a big statue. There is a stone table in front of the statue. And there is a stone chest on the table. On top of the chest, there is a shiny crystal ball.

Dan – Wow ! Look at that! Maybe this is Goddess Sekmet's room.

Claudia – Let's get out of here, Dan. I'm afraid. Maybe this is a sacred place.

Dan – You're right. It isn't safe here. Let's go.

But Claudia and Dan are trapped. The two men are behind them.

Doctor Jungen – Well, well, well. Look who's here – our little friends.

Godron – This is the end for you, kids. Pyramids are not safe places for children. Ha! Ha! Ha!

Claudia and Dan are terrified. They are in a corner of the room and they can't move. They're paralyzed with fear.

Doctor Jungen – This is Sekhmet's Room, Godron. It's the room of the papyrus, my papyrus.

Godron – Quick, Doctor! Let's take the papyrus and get out of here.

Chapter 3

The thieves are in front of the chest.

Godron – What's that, Doctor?

Doctor Jungen – It's a crystal ball, a kind of talisman. Let's take it with us.

Godron – It's too heavy! Help me.

Suddenly, there is a loud noise.

Godron – What's that noise, Dr Jungen?

Doctor Jungen – The floor, Godron! It's a trap! Help!

Doctor Jungen and Godron fall into the trap. They are killed instantly.

Claudia – Are you okay, Dan?

Dan – Sure, but let's get out of here. Quick!

Claudia – No! Wait. The papyrus is very important and the crystal ball is its only protection. Let's put the ball back in place.

Claudia and Dan put the ball on top of the chest. Suddenly, they hear a loud noise and the hole in the floor closes up.

Chapter 4

The two kids are leaving the room, when...
...they hear a voice.

Sekhmet – Wait, my children. I'm Sekhmet, goddess of power and war. I'm the guardian of the chest. Thanks to you, the papyrus is safe. The revelations contained in the papyrus are very important. But the men of your time are selfish and greedy. With the papyrus in their hands, they can destroy the world. But there is hope. The only hope is in people like you. You are pure at heart and honest. Now, go! Someday, the world will be ready for our secret. But not now... Now, this is our secret, a secret between you and me.

The group of tourists is outside the Great Pyramid now. Some are on the bus and others are still near the pyramid. They are talking.

Mrs Arnold – This pyramid is amazing!

Mr Lima – Yeah! And we're very lucky. Now we know everything about it.

Dan and Claudia – Well, not quite everything. Not yet.

Mrs Arnold – Not everything? How come?

Claudia and Dan – Well... That's our little secret.

KEY WORDS

The meaning of each word corresponds to its use in the context of the story (see page number 00)

according to (8) de acordo com
afraid (10) com medo
all (10) tudo
almost (9) quase
amazing (20) maravilhoso
angry (9) bravo
behind (4) atrás
between (19) entre
chamber (4) câmara
chest (13) baú
close up, closes up (17) fechar
contained (9) contido
corner (15) canto
corridor (4) corredor
crystal (13) cristal
dangerous (5) perigoso
dark (7) escuro
destroy (19) destruir
empty (10) vazio
fear (15) medo
floor (17) chão
footprint (7) pegada
gentleman (3) senhor
goddess (19) deusa
greedy (19) ganancioso
guardian (19) guardiã
heart (19) coração
heavy (16) pesado
hole (10) buraco
hope (19) esperança
huge (13) enorme
inside (4) dentro
instantly (17) instantaneamente
killed (17) morto
lady, ladies (3) senhora(s)
left (4) esquerda
loud (16) alto
lucky (20) sortudos
maybe (5) talvez
narrow (7) estreito
near (20) perto
nearby (12) por perto
noise (16) barulho
only (17) única
opening (6) abertura
outside (20) do lado de fora
papyrus (9) papiro
paralyzed (15) paralisado
passage (6) passagem
power (9) poder
push (7) empurrar
puzzled (6) confuso
quick (12) rápido
ray (11) raio
right (4) direita
room (10) sala
round (8) redondo
sacred (13) sagrado

safe (13) seguro
secret (6) secreto **(19)** segredo
selfish (19) egoísta
shiny (13) brilhante
small (4) pequeno(a)
shine, shines (10) brilhar
statue (13) estátua
suddenly (10) de repente
talisman (16) talismã
terrified (15) aterrorizado
thieve, thieves (9) ladrão, ladrões
through (10) através
tiny (10) minúsculo
trap (17) armadilha
trapped (14) presas
valley (3) vale
voice (7) voz
wall (7) parede
world (19) mundo

Expressions

Are you okay? (17) Você está bem?
Be quiet! (9) Fique quieto!
Don't worry! (5) Não se preocupe!
How come? (20) Como?
in trouble (9) em apuros
Let's go! (5) Vamos!
Not yet. (20) Ainda não.
We're close. (8) Estamos perto.
What about you? (3) E você?
Turn around! (11) Vire-se!

Before Reading

1. What do you know about the pyramids? Try to answer these questions in groups.
   a) Who built the pyramids?
   b) Where are the pyramids located?
   c) How old are the pyramids?
   d) Why were the pyramids built?

While Reading

Chapter 1

2. Who said what? Write C (Claudia) or D (Dan).
   a) (   ) I'm American.
   b) (   ) Maybe there's a secret door.
   c) (   ) Where are you from?
   d) (   ) I'm from Brazil.
   e) (   ) Isn't it dangerous?

3. Circle the words used to describe the things that are inside the pyramid.

corridor	bus	vacation	group	chamber	
door	valley	footprints	wall	window	light

Chapter 2

4. Answer the questions below.
   a) What is Dr Jungen's occupation?
   b) Where are Dr Jungen and his assistant Godron?
   c) Why are Claudia and Dan afraid?
   d) How does the sun help Claudia and Dan?

5. Match the columns to form expressions that appear in the story.

A	B
small	room
crystal	chamber
great	door
big	room
empty	moment
round	ball
huge	statue

Chapter 3

6. Choose the best alternative.
   1) Dr Jungen and Godron are:
      a) thieves   b) students
   2) The protection of the papyrus is:
      a) the chest   b) the crystal ball

Chapter 4

7. True or False?
   a) (   ) Sekhmet is the goddess of power and war.
   b) (   ) The papyrus is not very important.
   c) (   ) Men are nice and kind.
   d) (   ) The goddess thinks Claudia and Dan are pure at heart.
   e) (   ) All the tourists are in the bus.
   f) (   ) Mr Lima knows everything about the pyramid.

After Reading (Optional Activities)

8. In chapter 2, Doctor Jungen wants the papyrus to have the power of the Pharaohs. Why does he want this power?

9. In the last chapter, Sekhmet says that the men of our time are selfish and greedy. Can you think of recent events which show us this?

10. In your opinion, do the men in the story receive the right punishment? How do you think people like this should be punished?